From Rags to Riches: The Oprah Winfrey Story

CELEBRITY BIOGRAPHY BOOKS

Children's Biography Books

Speedy Publishing LLC
40 E. Main St. #1156
Newark, DE 19711
www.speedypublishing.com

Copyright © 2017

All Rights reserved. No part of this book may be reproduced or used in any way or form or by any means whether electronic or mechanical, this means that you cannot record or photocopy any material ideas or tips that are provided in this book.

In this book, we're going to talk about the amazing life of talk show host and actress Oprah Winfrey. So, let's get right to it!

WHO IS OPRAH WINFREY?

Oprah Winfrey is a legendary talk show host who had her own show called The Oprah Winfrey Show and who launched her own television network, The Oprah Winfrey Network (OWN). She's also a best-selling author, publisher, producer, and a philanthropist, which means that she gives lots of her money away to charities.

Oprah giving a speech.

Oprah Winfrey signature / logo

To date, she's the only African-American billionaire in the United States. She came from very humble beginnings and is completely self-made. Her passion and drive are what brought her to the pinnacle of success.

EARLY LIFE

Oprah was born in the state of Mississippi in a city called Kosciusko. Her mother Vernita Lee was just a teenager when she had Oprah. Her father, a United States army private, was Vernon Winfrey. Her parents weren't married.

New Orleans Mississippi River.

Oprah's mom wanted to name her after a Bible character in the Book of Ruth from the Old Testament. The name of the character was "Orpah," but it was misspelled as Oprah and that was Oprah's interesting name from then on.

Oprah Winfrey in Denmark in 2009.

TV presenter/actress Oprah Winfrey.

HUMBLE BEGINNINGS

Oprah had a troubled childhood. When Oprah was still a child, her mom had to move to Wisconsin to look for employment. Oprah's grandmother, Hattie Mae, took over as Oprah's guardian for the time being. Hattie Mae had a farm in Mississippi and Oprah was responsible for a lot of the farm chores. The farm didn't have any plumbing, so Oprah carried the water from the well to the house every day. This was a big task for a child who wasn't even six years old yet.

Oprah Winfrey at the 2002 Emmy Awards.

Oprah's grandmother taught Oprah to read and write from the age of three. They read the Bible together. They were so poor that Oprah sometimes dressed in potato sacks and was made fun of by the local children. Her grandmother was strict and believed in discipline, but she also encouraged Oprah to be self confident and sure of herself. Her grandmother recalled that Oprah used to play at interviewing her corncob dolls and the black crows that frequented the farm's fields and fences.

Oprah Winfrey at the 30th Annual People's Choice Awards in Pasadena, CA. January 11, 2004.

Eventually, at the age of six, Oprah moved north to Wisconsin where her mom was working. Oprah's mom was living in poverty so life was very difficult. Her mom had trouble with drugs and Oprah was a wild child as a teenager. She was bounced around from her mom to her dad during her childhood and adolescent years. Sometimes her mom had a hard time disciplining her, so Oprah lived with her dad in Tennessee for a while.

TV chat show queen Oprah Winfrey & fiance Stedman Graham.

Her dad made her education a priority and Oprah's earlier reading and writing lessons at her grandmother's farm paid off. She was an excellent student and understood early on that education would be a path for success. She soaked up books and loved to read. In 1971, despite all her difficulties growing up, she graduated with honors from East Nashville High School.

A GIFTED SPEAKER

As a young girl, Oprah enjoyed being the center of attention. Most people really dislike public speaking, but Oprah loved it. She grabbed every opportunity to speak in public and was fearless about giving presentations at church, at school, and for different women's groups.

An image of Oprah Winfrey in Shadow Ink App.

While she was still in high school, she participated in and won a speaking contest. The award was a full scholarship to attend college and she decided to attend Tennessee State University.

Oprah Winfrey visits evacuees from New Orleans temporarily sheltered at the Reliant center in Houston following Hurricane Katrina.

When she was 17 years old, she entered a beauty pageant to be named "Miss Black Tennessee." She was the pageant winner and when she was interviewed after the pageant she mentioned that she wanted to go into broadcasting. She caught the attention of the local radio station WVOL that had an African-American audience.

Times Square billboards with Oprah Winfrey and Bank of America.

She read the news as a part-time job there during her senior year in high school and she continued the job during her first two years attending college. She loved her job and was on her way to a profitable career.

NEWS ANCHOR JOB IN NASHVILLE

While she was still in college, Oprah received an important phone call. It was from the CBS news station located in Nashville. They wanted to offer her the news anchor position. It was a like a dream come true for Oprah. She couldn't believe that it was happening.

Oprah Winfrey at the 19th Annual Critics' Choice Awards at The Barker Hangar, Santa Monica Airport.

She was conflicted though because she couldn't start the job and also stay in school. In the end it was too good of an opportunity to pass up. When she took the

Historic interview of Oprah Winfrey by Dave Letterman.

position she was only 19 years old and at that time she was the very first female news anchor that was African-American in the city's history.

HER FIRST TALK SHOW

In 1976, Oprah traveled from Nashville to Baltimore, Maryland to take a job at a TV station there. She was working as a news anchor, but it wasn't quite the right fit for her. Then, she was moved to a television talk show format. The show was called "People Are Talking" and it was a match made in heaven for her.

Oprah Winfrey arrives at the Oprah Winfrey Network Winter 2011 TCA Party.

An issue of Oprah's magazine.

Oprah said later that her first day on the job felt as easy as breathing. The show was a local hit and Winfrey was its host for eight years, during which she developed her own style.

Photo of Johnny Carson and Phil Donahue from Donahue's syndicated television talk program, The Phil Donahue Show.

Then, a Chicago television station pursued her to host their morning program called A.M. Chicago. At that time, Phil Donahue's program was their major competitor. Phil was very popular and no one suspected what would happen next. Within just a few months, Oprah won over more viewers. She soon had 100,000 more viewers than Donahue and had taken a show that was in last place to first place.

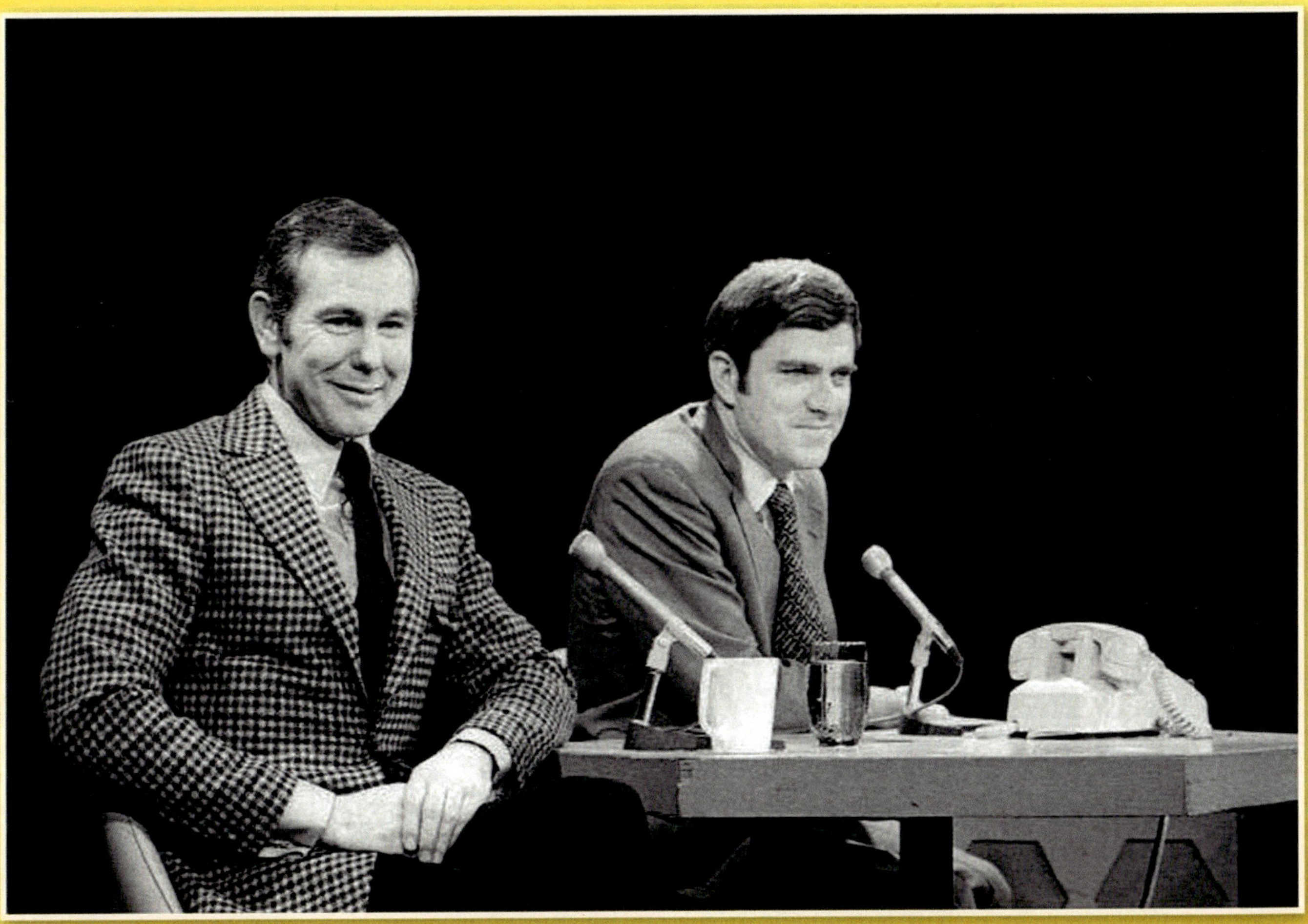

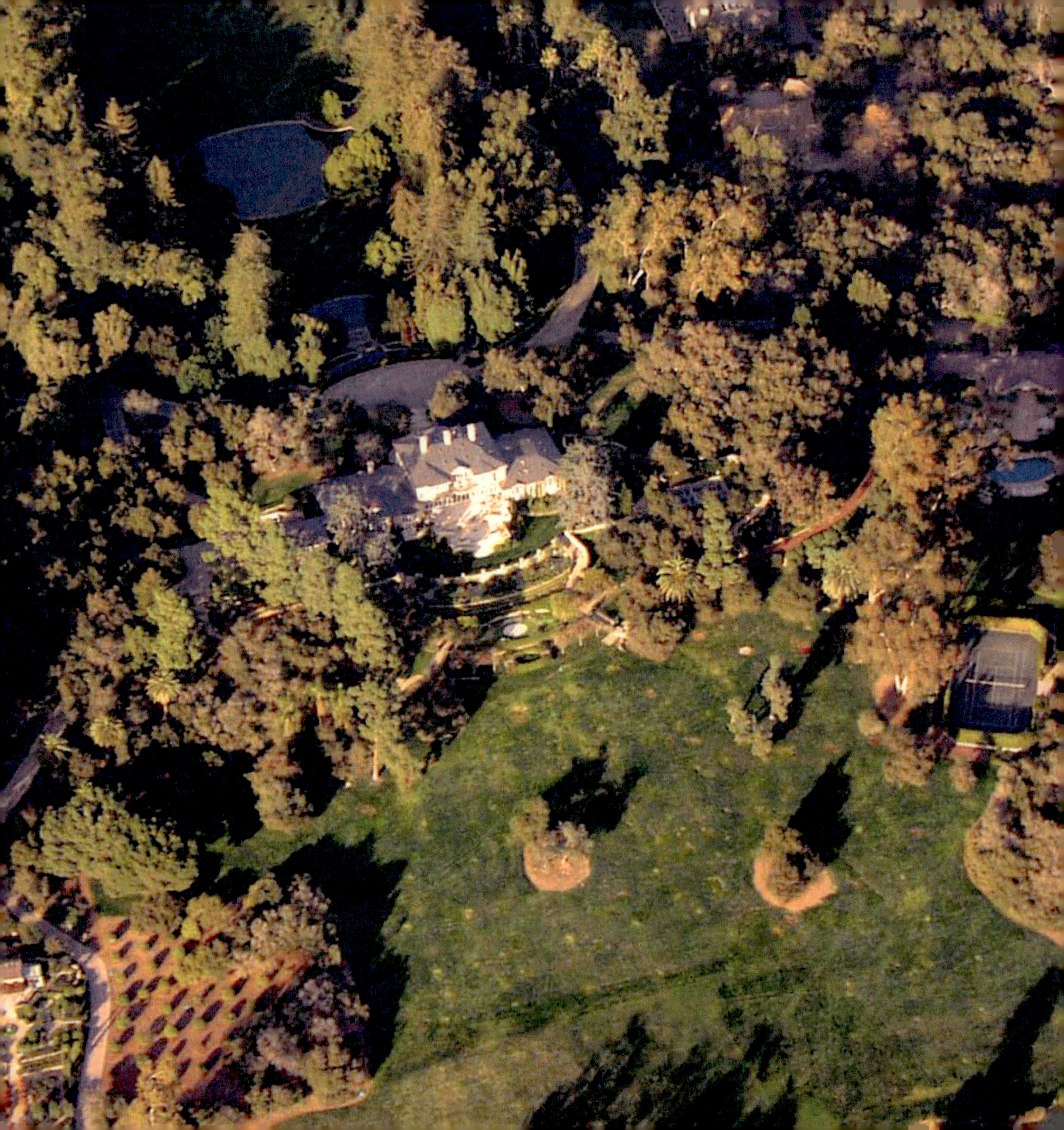

Oprah's estate.

A large portion of her success had to do with the fact that she wasn't afraid to talk about her own personal problems and challenges on the air. Women and men of all ages and races identified with her warm-hearted and personal way of interviewing the guests who came on her program.

Oprah being hugged by First Lady Michelle Obama.

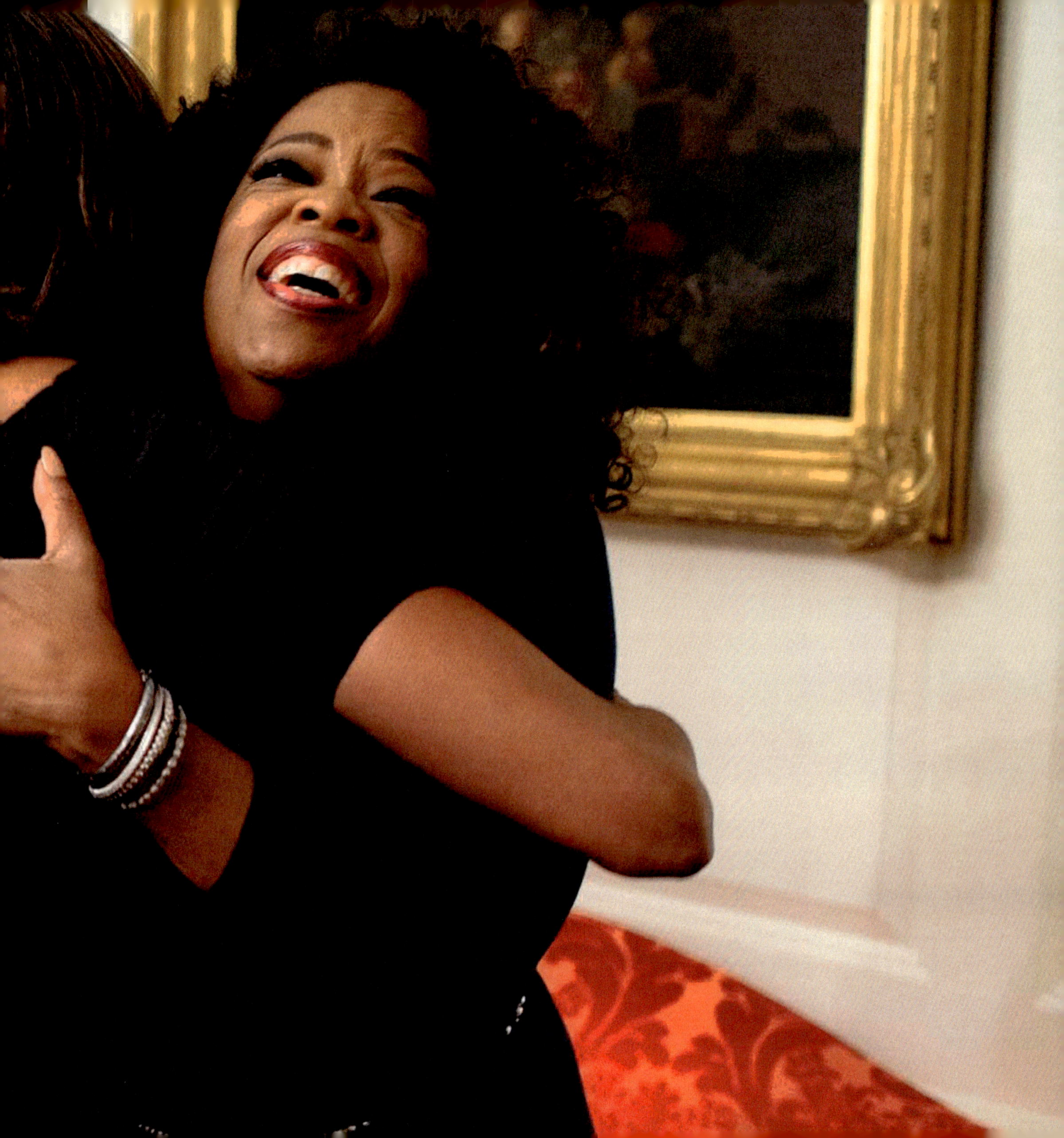

The Color Purple poster.

THE COLOR PURPLE

Then, another interesting opportunity happened for Oprah. Her fame had made her known and she had the chance to audition for a part in the Steven Spielberg film, The Color Purple, which was to be made in 1985. Oprah loved the book so much, but after she auditioned nothing happened and she was so disappointed. She kept thinking about it.

Steven Spielberg.

The casting agent had told her she "wasn't an actress" and it was bothering her. She had just made a decision to mentally let it go when Spielberg's office called to tell her that they wanted her for the part. She was nominated for an Academy Award for her supporting role and she has said that the opportunity changed her life.

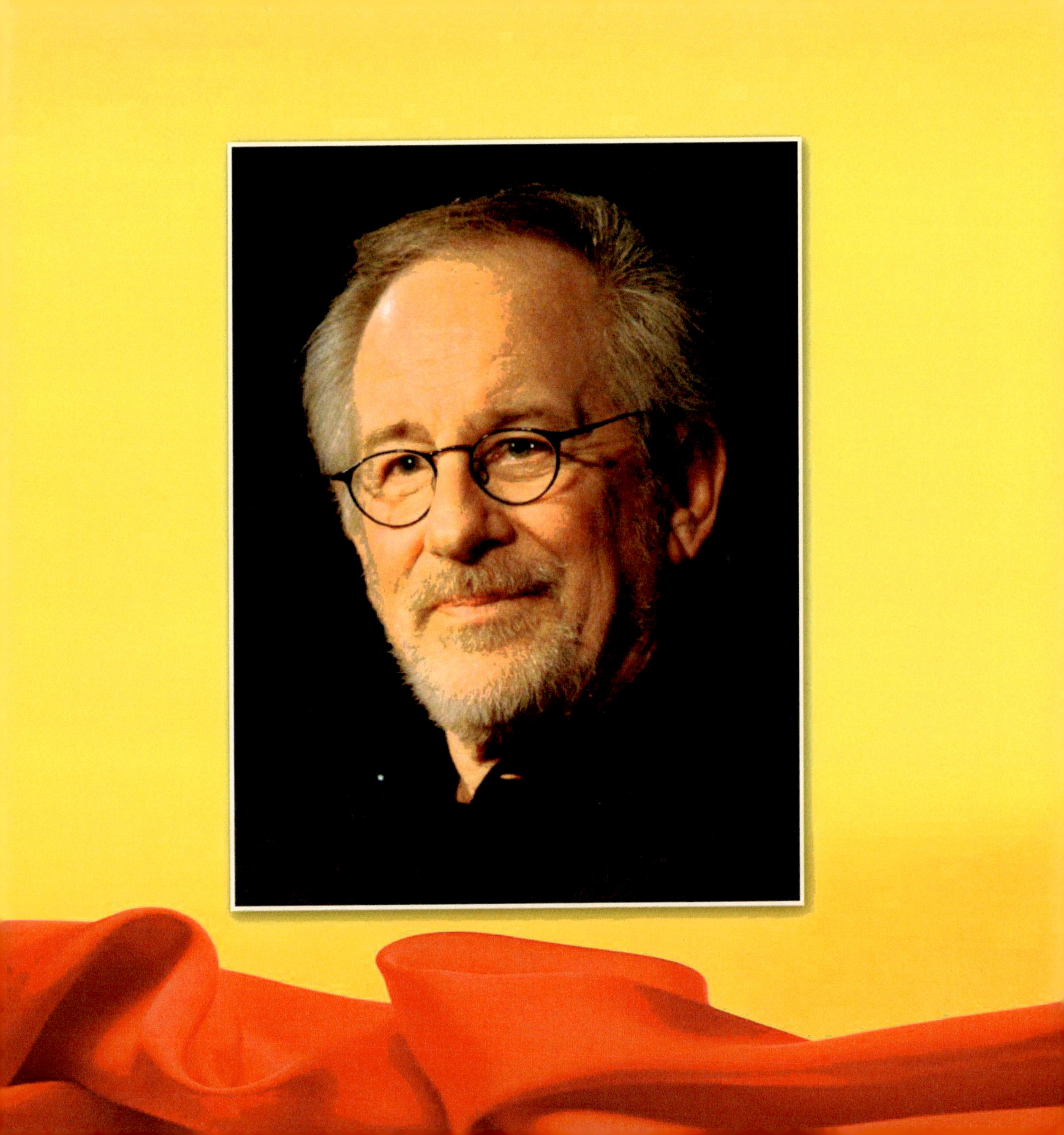

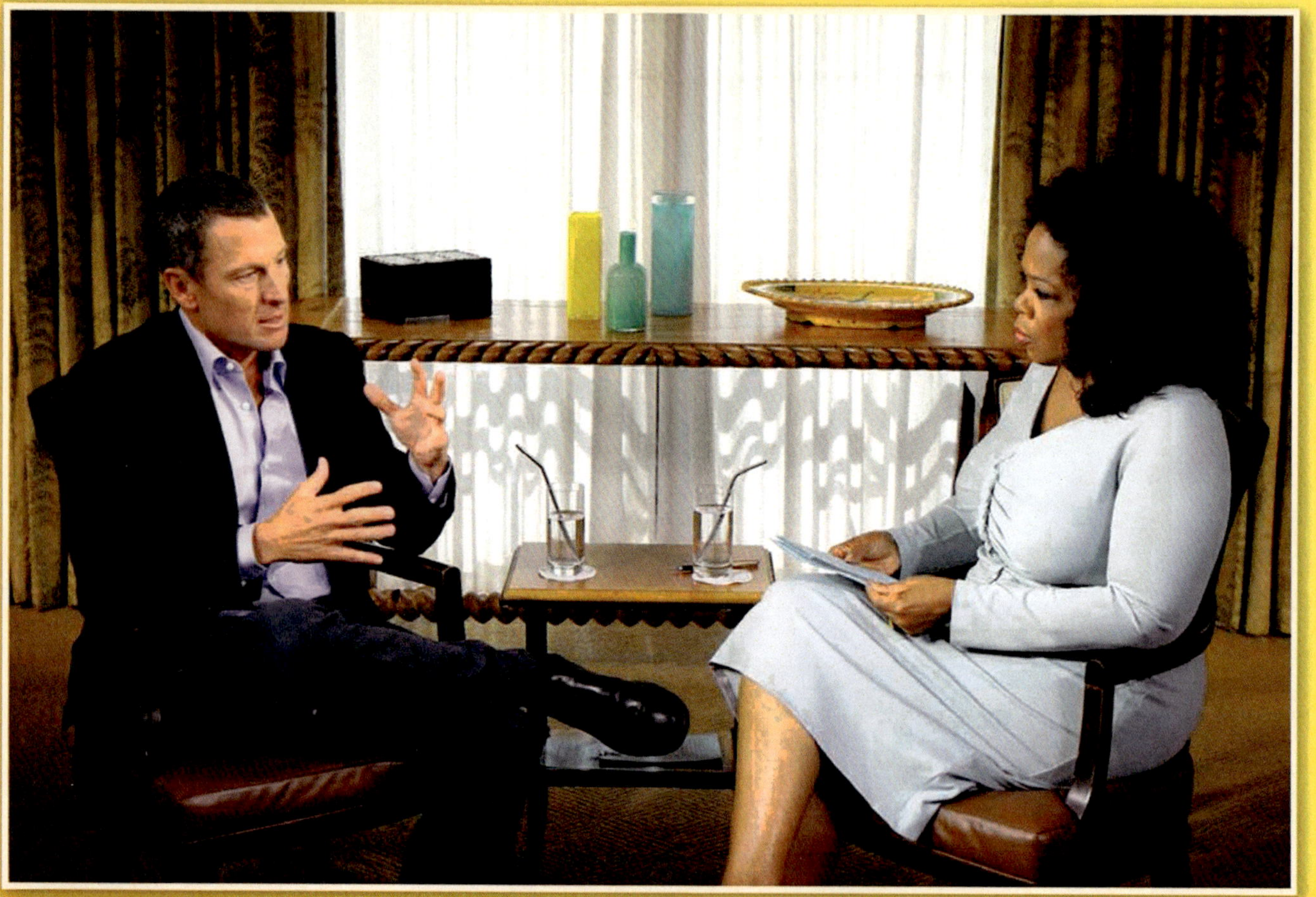

Oprah interiewing Lance Armstrong.

She played the role of Sofia who was married to Harpo, which Oprah noticed was her name spelled backwards. Over the years, Oprah has acted in a few other select projects including the movies, The Women of Brewster Place in 1989 and The Butler in 2013.

THE OPRAH WINFREY SHOW

In 1986, Oprah launched her own show, which was named after her. It was syndicated, which means that it ran on many channels at the same time. Her show was soon running on 120 different channels and her audience quickly grew to a population of over 10 million viewers. By the end of the first year it was on the air, the show had earned over $125 million dollars and Oprah was earning a salary of over $30 million.

Oprah Winfrey Harpo Studios Sign in Chicago.

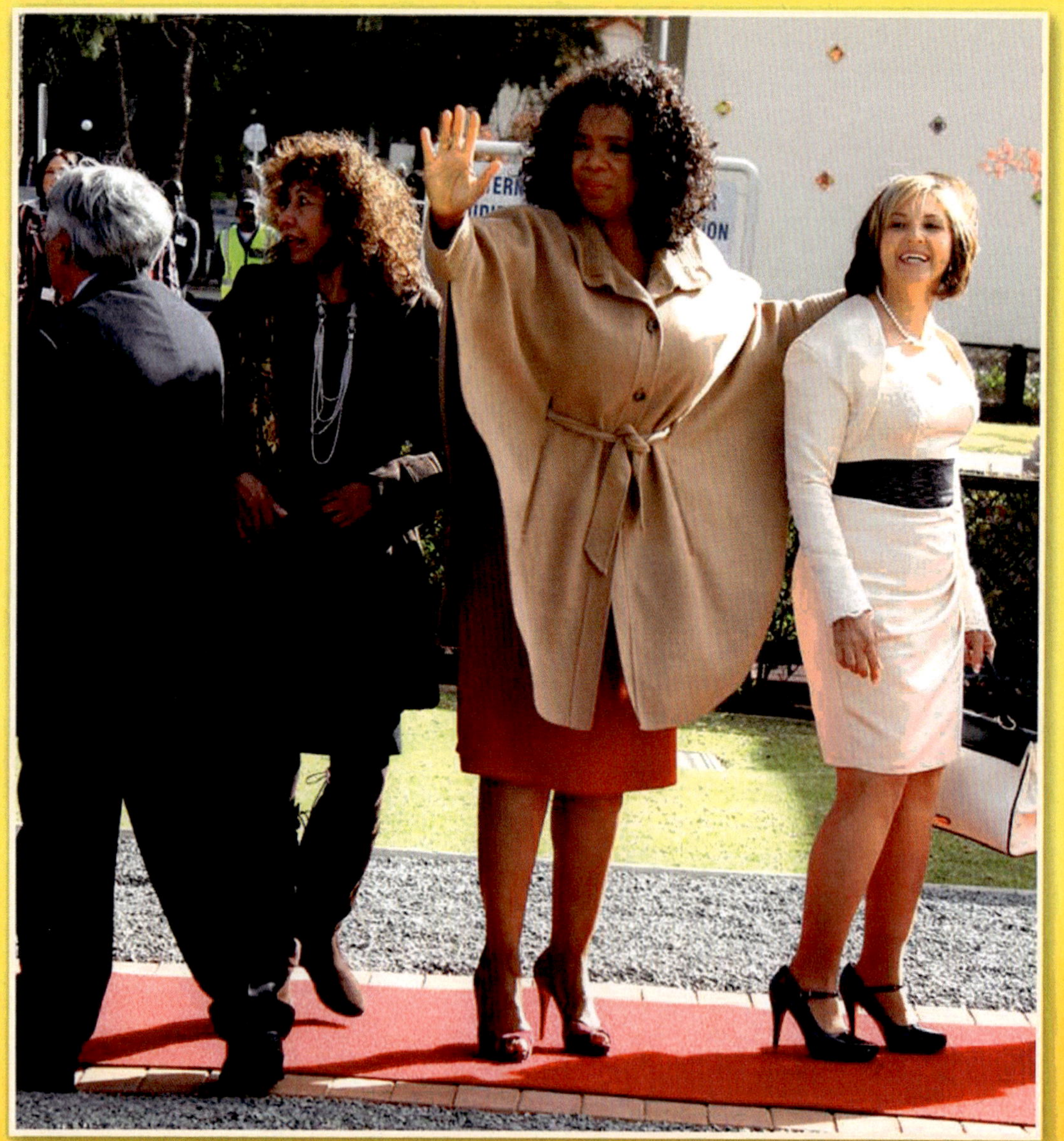

Oprah Winfrey visiting the University of the Free in Bloemfontein, Free State.

She was on her way to becoming a very rich woman. She eventually gained total control over the show with the production company she created, which she named Harpo Productions. Her show was on the air for a record-breaking 25 years and wrapped its final episode in 2011. Her book club was instrumental in revitalizing a love for reading across the country and helped many authors get the word out about their books.

BRANCHING OUT

Through the years, Oprah's brand has become a media empire. She was one of the founders of the Oxygen Media cable TV company and launched her own magazine, which she called O. In 2009, she started her own network for television programming named the Oprah Winfrey Network and abbreviated as OWN.

OWN
OPRAH WINFREY NETWORK

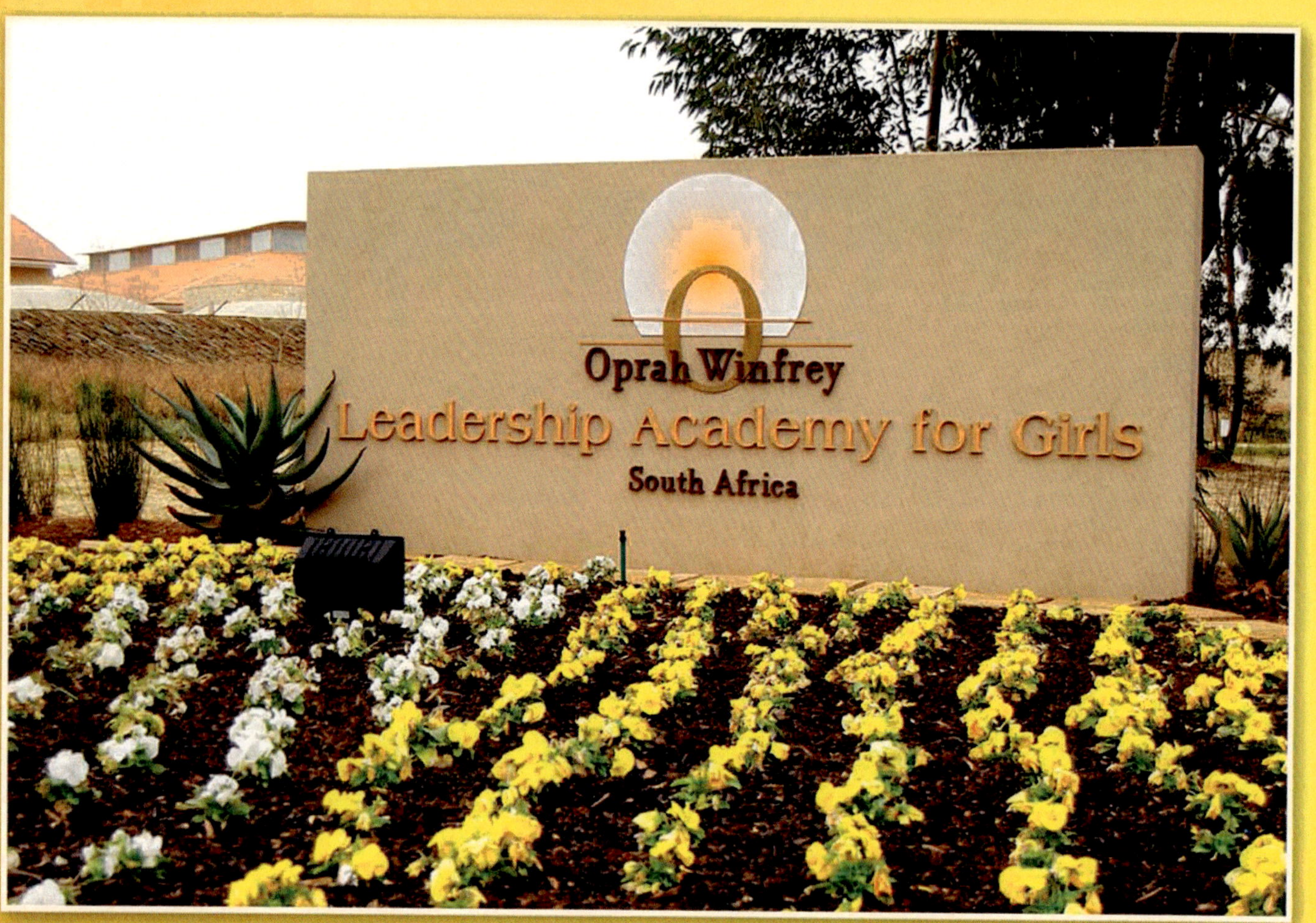
Oprah Winfrey
Leadership Academy for Girls
South Africa

PHILANTHROPY

Oprah has a special charity network called Oprah's Angel Network. She has raised and given out more than $51 million dollars for a variety of charitable causes including education of girls in South Africa and relief to Hurricane Katrina victims.

Oprah Winfrey Leadership Academy for Girls.

President Obama Honors Presidential Medal of Freedom Recipient Oprah Winfrey.

In November of 2013, President Obama awarded her the highest honor a civilian can receive in the US, the Presidential Medal of Freedom. It was given to her for the contributions she's made to charity and the role model she's become for others who grew up in poverty.

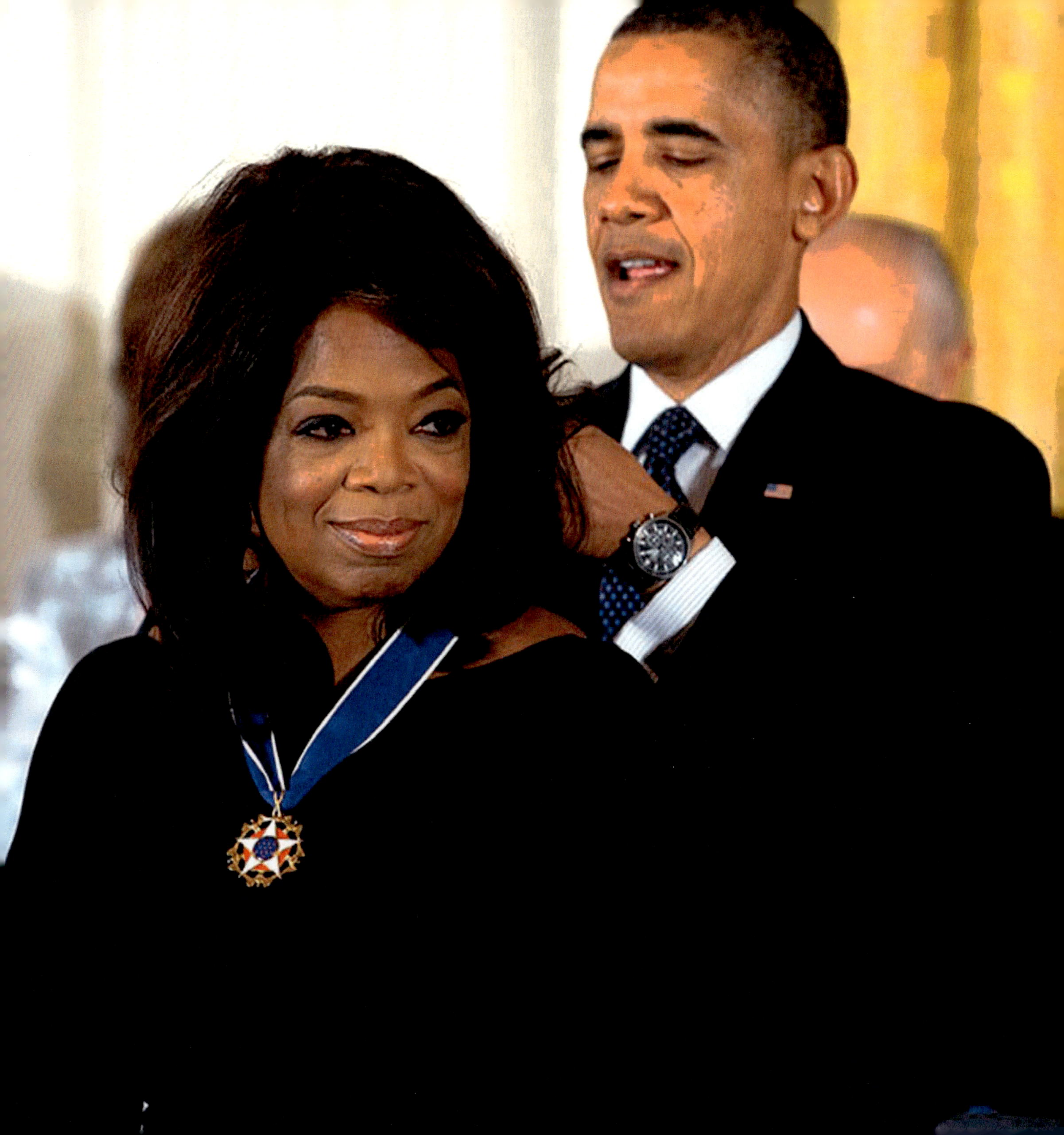

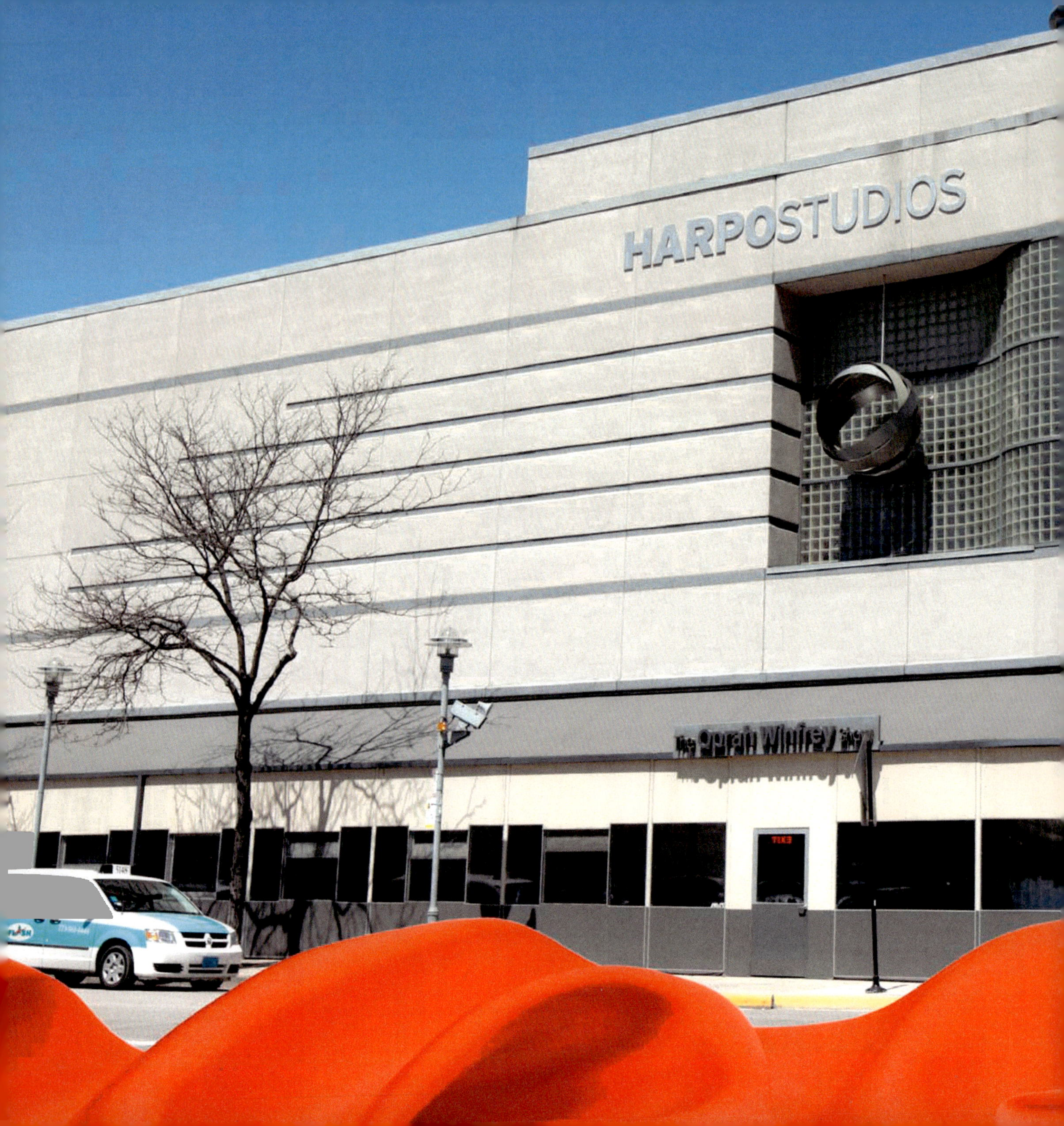
HARPOSTUDIOS
The Oprah Winfrey Show

Awesome! Now you know more about the life and achievements of Oprah Winfrey. You can find more Biography books from Baby Professor by searching the website of your favorite book retailer.

Harpo Studios in Chicago.

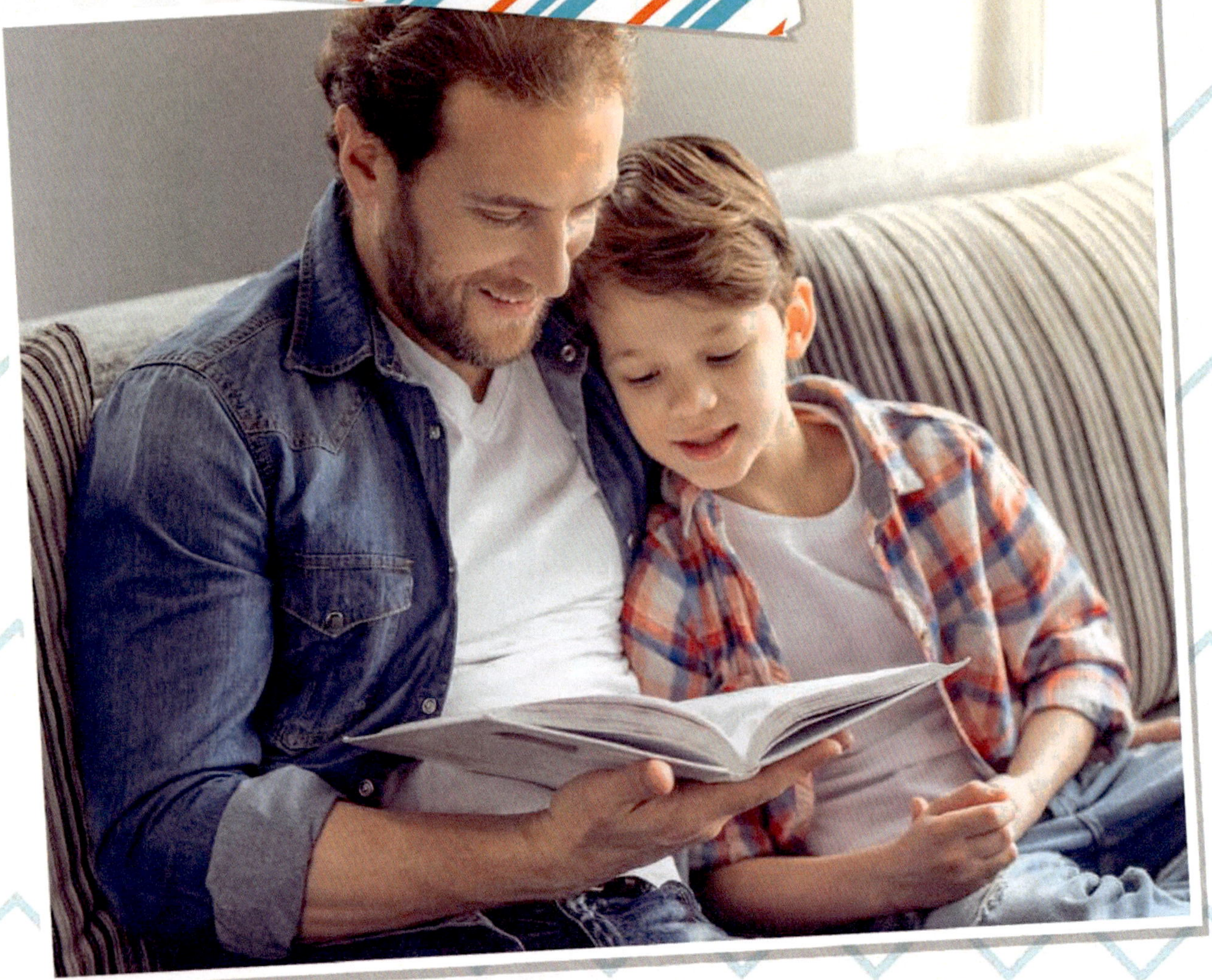

Visit

BABY PROFESSOR
EDUCATION KIDS

www.BabyProfessorBooks.com

to download Free Baby Professor eBooks and view our catalog of new and exciting Children's Books